I MATTER

*Love Yourself Unconditionally
and Nurture Your Self-Worth*

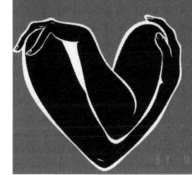

A GUIDE TO BE
A BETTER SPOUSE
A BETTER PARENT
A BETTER YOU!

BY MYKAL COLES.

iMatter – A Guide to Self Love by Mykal Coles

Table of Contents

Introduction

What is self-love? We can think of it as a desire to give our own well-being a level of importance and respect. If you love yourself, you have regard for yourself. It's about treating yourself as well as you would treat anyone you love.

But most of us have been conditioned to believe that we should put ourselves last. We do this under the guise of caring about others or modesty. However, this is very self-defeating. You can't do as much for others when you don't make yourself a priority, too.

"Love yourself first and everything else falls into line. You really have to love yourself to get anything done in this world."

– LUCILLE BALL

You must live with yourself every minute of the day, so you may as well enjoy your company!

Consider these topics as a means to learn to love and appreciate yourself:

1. Chapter 1: Are you Using the Right Criteria to Measure Your Self-Worth? Having and utilizing the correct measuring stick makes a difference. We often judge ourselves by the culture in which we live. This can be a mistake.

2. Chapter 2: A 30-day Beginning to Self-Love. Many experts believe it takes 30 days to build a habit. Effective habits ensure your desired outcome. In 30 days, you can accomplish a lot and gain the momentum needed to make a real breakthrough in your self-love.

3. Chapter 3: Conclusion. This is just the beginning of your path to true self-love and self-esteem. Where will you go next?

"If only you could sense how important you are to the lives of those you meet; how important you can be to people you may never even dream of.

There is something of yourself that you leave at every meeting with another person."

- FRED ROGERS

Are you Using the Right Criteria to Measure Your Self-Worth?

How do you determine your self-worth? Is it how much money you have? The fact that you can fit into skinny jeans? A great job and a Mercedes? It's an interesting question. Most of us just have a vague notion of whether or not we should love ourselves given our circumstances in life.

A good thing to consider is how you think your child should measure their self-worth. Do you think a child should love themselves more or less if they were:

- Wealthy or poor?
- More or less attractive than the average person?
- Failed more times than they were successful?
- Succeeded more times than they failed?

Would you consider any of these to be a reason for a child to love themselves more or less? What criteria would you use?

Things that probably shouldn't determine your degree of self-love:

1. Your education. If your child decides to become a welder or a preschool teacher instead of going to college, would you consider them to have less worth? If you need to go to college to pursue your dreams, then go. If you don't, there's no reason to feel bad about not attending.

2. Your body shape or attractiveness. While your diet and exercise routine have a great effect on how you look, much of your appearance is out of your hands. The color of your eyes, your height, and your general body shape are determined by your genes.

   - Consider your spouse, child, friend, or even a pet you love. If their appearance took a turn for the worse, would you think less of them? Of course not. So, there's no reason to think less of yourself for not looking like a fitness model or movie star.

3. Your career. Some careers are more challenging or lucrative than others. But there's more to life than splitting atoms or making six figures.

   - If you enjoy what you do, can pay your bills, and have enough time and money left over to do the things you love, you're doing incredibly well.

4. Your financial situation. Happiness is a more worthy goal than wealth. Studies show that happiness doesn't increase beyond the $70k/year mark. Having more money than that doesn't matter much.

    - If you're making less than that, it might be worth your while to reach that level. However, your income says nothing about how much you should love yourself. There have been many spectacular people that never made a lot of money.

5. Your possessions. If you travel, you'll notice how people in the US and Canada compare to those in most other countries. We're obsessed with having more. Interestingly, people from many relatively poor countries often rate themselves as happier than the people in North America.

    - There will always be someone with more. It's a battle you can't win.

6. Your successes and failures. Everyone has successes and failures. You can always try again. The most successful people have often had the most spectacular failures. If anything, you might have a good reason to be happy with yourself for failing a lot.

7. The people you know. Are you more worthy of self-love because of whom you know? Are you any less worthy of self-love because of whom you don't know?

- Things outside of you can't be a valid determiner of your self-worth. It's called "self" for a reason.

This list might seem a little daunting since these are the very things that are prized by many in our culture. However, if you want to love yourself, it's important to use valid criteria.

The keys to loving yourself are to know yourself and to be on a path to become a person that you respect. You're already amazing. Realizing that is half the battle.

The other part is to see regular improvement in yourself. Humans are happiest when making progress. You get to determine what that progress is moving toward. You'll be more pleased with yourself if you start working on those things that you think are important.

Our society thinks that certain things are important. However, your self-worth is independent of where you live. Why would you like yourself more or less if you lived in Ukraine, Hawaii, or Australia? You're still the same person. Society can't give you permission to love yourself or take it away from you.

"Remember always that you not only have the right to be an individual, you have an obligation to be one."

- ELEANOR ROOSEVELT

Chapter 2:
A 30-Day Beginning to Self-Love

Thirty days is enough time to see progress for most endeavors. It's long enough to lose a few pounds or to increase the number of pushups you can do. You can hit a tennis ball much better after a month. You can even learn to play a simple tune on the violin.

It's also enough time to increase your ability to love yourself. In 30 days, you can discover how wonderful you are.

You can also begin to learn how to treat yourself well and put yourself on the road to self-improvement. But this self-improvement has nothing to do with gaining the things society values. It's about becoming the type of person you most admire.

Many of these items can be done daily. It's important to create habits of these items. Self-love is largely the result of your habits. The right habits will create the outcome you're looking for.

A few of these items aren't practical to do every day unless you're retired. Think of those as weekly or monthly tasks.

Consider this a 30-day self-love challenge. Keep an open mind and have the courage to complete it. You'll be glad you did!

Day 0:

Set Your Intention for the Next 30 Days

It's much easier to accomplish something when you have an intention. Your vegetable garden didn't get planted last summer by accident. You had the intention of planting it. The same concept applies here.

Avoid wasting the next 30 days. Decide that you're going to work on your self-love and self-esteem for a month. Be determined to give the next month your best effort. It's challenging to change your daily routine, and you have much to accomplish.

Your intention and determination are paramount to your success.

"A healthy self-love means we have no compulsion to justify to ourselves or others why we take vacations, why we sleep late, why we buy new shoes, why we spoil ourselves from time to time. We feel comfortable doing things which add quality and beauty to life."

- ANDREW MATTHEWS

Day 1:
Become Aware

It's difficult to make progress without understanding where you are currently. Begin noticing the way you treat yourself. Then, contrast that with how you treat your friends and family.

Most of us are more patient, understanding, and tolerant of others than we are of ourselves. In fact, most of us treat complete strangers better than we treat ourselves!

Notice your tendencies regarding how you treat yourself. Pay particular attention to these areas:

- Self-talk

- How you feel when you make a mistake versus how you feel when someone else makes a mistake

- Does the way you treat yourself encourage you to be your best?

- Do you treat yourself as if you're important and worthy of respect?

- Are the ways you think and act toward yourself habitual?

Spend the next 30 days with a greater level of awareness regarding your attitude and behavior toward yourself.

Day 2:
Accept All the Compliments that Come Your Way

When you're short on self-love, it's not easy to accept compliments. Do you feel uncomfortable when someone singles you out in a positive way? While modesty is generally a good policy to follow, it's okay to feel happy about receiving a compliment.

Starting today, accept all the compliments that others give you. A quick smile and a thank you is enough. Tell yourself that you deserve it. Avoid giving in to any temptation to deflect.

"People may flatter themselves just as much by thinking that their faults are always present to other people's minds, as if they believe that the world is always contemplating their individual charms and virtues."

- ELIZABETH GASKELL

Day 3:
Start Reading a Book on the Topic of Self-Love

For the remainder of the 30 days, spend at least 15 minutes each day reading a book on the topic of self-love. If you get finished, start a new book. In lieu of a book, read an article online. Find a credible source and learn all you can about the importance and the process of self-love.

Here are a couple of ideas:

- *The Self-Love Experiment: Fifteen Principles for Becoming More Kind, Compassionate, and Accepting of Yourself* by Shannon Kaiser

- *Self Love: Achieve Lasting Self Love with Positive Thinking, Unconditional Confidence, and Unshakeable Self Esteem* by Karen Roe

Regardless of your source material, give the information you learn some thought. Ask yourself how you can incorporate it into your life.

Day 4:
Create and Use Affirmations

Affirmations take time to work, so it's a good thing you have a few weeks ahead of you to allow the power of affirmations to work for you. With enough repetition, you can get yourself to believe nearly anything. Advertisers work from this mindset, and considering how much we purchase, it's can't be too far off the mark!

Use these strategies daily to enable affirmations to reprogram your subconscious for greater self-love:

1. Create 10 affirmations that address self-love. Remember that in day one you've been increasing your awareness of your behavior and attitude toward yourself. Create affirmations that take this new information into account.

- Affirmations should be positive and direct.
- "I love myself completely" is an example of an affirmation.

2. Carry your affirmations with you. You can have a copy on your phone, in a small notebook, or on an index card. Whatever you'll consistently carry with you is fine.

3. Read your affirmations several times each day. Whenever you have a spare moment, pull out your affirmations and read them. Try reading them to yourself and aloud when appropriate. Begin and end your day with your affirmations.

"You have been criticizing yourself for years, and it hasn't worked. Try approving of yourself and see what happens."

- LOUISE L. HAY

Day 5:
Do Something You've Always Wanted To Do

Splurge on yourself a little today. Maybe you've always wanted a hot stone massage, to try Vietnamese food, or learn to ride a motorcycle. Spend a little time and think about it. Then, go out and make it happen. If you need to wait for the weekend, make concrete plans for your activity and stick to them.

Day 6:

Admire Your Body

You might be lacking a six-pack, have added a few wrinkles over the years, and wear bifocals, but those are small potatoes compared to what your body can still do. Even if your health is quite poor, you can still do some amazing things.

Consider the things many of us take for granted:

- The ability to see, hear, smell, touch, and taste. Consider how much pleasure these senses provide.

- The ability to walk and talk. How many amazing things can you experience just by having these two abilities?

- Maybe you've created children.

You might think that your body isn't much to look at anymore, but that's a small issue. When you consider how much that body can still do, the other stuff is irrelevant.

"There are days I drop words of comfort on myself like falling leaves and remember that it is enough to be taken care of by myself."

- BRIAN ANDREAS

Day 7:
Eat Nutritiously

Prove to yourself that you love your body by treating it like a king or queen for a day. Instead of giving in to your regular habits and impulses, eat nutritiously for just one day.

Feel free to continue for the remainder of the month, or even the rest of your life.

Day 8:
Send Yourself a Love Letter

Imagine you had the most perfect friend or partner. Write yourself a letter from that person. Be loving and encouraging. You can write it on paper, send yourself an email, or even leave a voicemail. It's up to you. You might even consider turning this into a daily habit.

Day 9:
Ask Someone for a Favor

Those lacking in self-love don't like to be bothersome to others. But, asking for help isn't bothersome. You'd help someone else, so it's only reasonable to assume that others would be happy to help you, too. You're important and deserve help when you need it.

Think of something that you could use some help with and ask an appropriate person for their help. Start small and build your comfort level.

Day 10:
Remove the Need for Perfection

Whether you require perfection from yourself, others, or both, you can bet you're consistently miserable. Perfection doesn't truly exist. It's a theoretical idea that can never be attained.

You might believe you've met the perfect man or woman. But you haven't. You just haven't experienced the imperfections yet.

When you demand perfection from yourself, you can never be happy with yourself. This is a perfect way to always be disgruntled and resent yourself. Setting impossible expectations can never lead to satisfaction.

Be kind to yourself and realize that your best effort is enough. Spend today relieving yourself of the need to be perfect.

"I found in my research that the biggest reason people aren't more self-compassionate is that they are afraid they'll become self-indulgent. They believe self-criticism is what keeps them in line. Most people have gotten it wrong because our culture says being hard on yourself is the way to be."

- KRISTEN NEFF

Day 11:
Declutter Your Home Environment

Most of us have way too much stuff in our homes. It creates stress and doesn't leave enough room for anything new to come into our lives. Cleaning and decluttering isn't necessarily fun, but it does provide a sense of control.

A clean, tidy environment is good for your self-esteem and peace of mind. Start with a single room today and branch out from there. Just a few minutes of decluttering each day can make a huge difference. Learn to keep things neat rather than waiting until the situation becomes unbearable before you take action.

Know that you deserve to live in a pleasant environment.

Day 12:
Clean Up Your Schedule

How much time do you spend doing things you don't want to do? Okay, we all have to do things we don't want to do, but there are things you don't want to do that you don't actually have to do. It might be serving on the Parent-Teacher Organization or playing on the company softball team.

Take a look at your average month and list the activities that you don't enjoy. Yes, you still have to pay your bills, but there are at least a few things on that list that you don't have to do.

So, don't do them. Let the appropriate people know, and then use that time for something that you do enjoy. Your happiness and time are important.

Day 13:
Develop a Strategy for Dealing With Stress

Many of the chronic challenges in life are a result of dealing with stress poorly. Whether it's irresponsible spending, overeating, passing on great opportunities, or worse, it's likely due to handling stress poorly.

Developing an effective, and healthy, method of dealing with stress can provide amazing benefits in your life.

Here are a few healthy options for dealing with stress effectively:

1. Meditate. Meditation has been around for thousands of years and has never been more popular than it is right now.

2. Exercise. Going for a short jog or doing a few pushups can make you feel a lot better. It's also good for you.

3. Call a friend. Reach out to someone that cares. Most of us have someone in our life that can always make us feel better.

4. Let it go. With practice, you can drop your stress just like you can drop a heavy suitcase.

5. Find a solution. If the cause of your stress can be managed, manage it instead of worrying about it.

Notice when you're feeling stressed and try one of these strategies. If you have an even better idea, feel free to try it.

"If you aren't good at loving yourself, you will have a difficult time loving anyone, since you'll resent the time and energy you give another person that you aren't even giving to yourself."

- BARBARA DE ANGELIS

Day 14:
Create a Gratitude List

Even if you're friendless and living on a park bench, there are still things in your life you can be grateful for. If you aren't sleeping in the rain, you have even more to be happy about.

Our culture focuses on the negative more than the positive. People that travel extensively often notice that people from North America spend a lot of time talking about what they don't like. But, people from other cultures often spend their time talking about what they do like.

You can create your own little culture and choose to focus on what's right in your life.

So, your task for today, and the remainder of the 30 days, is to make a list of everything you are grateful for in your life. List everything over the next month. Include your comfy couch, air conditioning, coffee, friends, and anything else you enjoy or value.

Day 15:
Exercise

Exercise is good for you, and hence, shows that you love yourself when you do it regularly. Exercise is beneficial for your stress levels, heart and lungs, muscles, and metabolism. It's also good for your self-esteem, and you'll look better, too.

Think of ways you can get some exercise and enjoy it. You might set up a regular walking date with a friend, take boxing lessons, or play golf.

The key to exercising consistently is to make a habit of it by scheduling time for it and enjoying it. When you enjoy doing something, it's easier to do it regularly.

How can you enjoy exercising? Think about it and make it happen.

"When I loved myself enough, I began leaving whatever wasn't healthy. This meant people, jobs, my own beliefs and habits – anything that kept me small. My judgement called it disloyal. Now I see it as self-loving."

- KIM MCMILLEN

Day 16:
Clean Up Your Social Life

We all have at least one person in our life that shouldn't be there. It might be an old high school friend that takes advantage of us, an old boyfriend or girlfriend that we should stay away from, or it might even be a family member that consistently mistreats you. Maybe you can't stand the guy at the deli counter.

Who is in your life that shouldn't be there?

- Make a list of everyone in your life. A spreadsheet would be perfect.

- Now order them from worst to best.

- Start chopping until you reach the people that are positive and meaningful in your life.

This might require a conversation. Or maybe you just need to stop responding to someone's text messages. Get it done. You're special and deserve to have special people in your life.

Day 17:
Do What You Love

How much of your time each day is spent actually doing something that you love? After rushing around in the morning getting ready for work, driving to work, working, and then driving home, a large part of the day is gone. And yet, you probably haven't spent any time doing something you enjoy.

If you wait until you have free time to do the things you love to do, you'll never do them. The key is to schedule time each day to do something you enjoy. The things you like to do are important, because you're important.

Schedule at least 30 minutes today, and each day going forward, to do something you enjoy. It doesn't matter how silly or meaningless it might be. If you enjoy it, that's enough.

"Self-pity gets you nowhere. One must have the adventurous daring to accept oneself as a bundle of possibilities and undertake the most interesting game in the world making the most of one's best."

- HARRY EMERSON FOSDICK

Day 18:
Make Plans for Your Future

It's not enough to just survive. That's what animals do. You're a human being with choices. Sit down with a cup of coffee or a glass of wine and plan your future. You deserve to have the life you desire.

Let your imagination run wild and create a compelling future. Put your plan on paper.

Most importantly, make a plan and do at least one thing each day to make it a reality. That means taking the first step today!

Day 19:
Keep a Journal

A life worth living is worth recording. You'll show yourself that your life is important enough to write down. You'll also begin to see the mistakes you make but are currently not aware of. Your life will also improve. After all, you won't want to write down the same thing each day. You'll be determined to do something worthy of recording.

Whether you choose to do it by hand or with a word processor is up to you. Start today and spend a few minutes each night recording your day and thoughts.

Day 20:
Forgive Yourself

You've done plenty of things wrong. Some of them were even intentional. Take comfort in the fact that everyone you know has done the same. You've lived and learned. It's time to let it go and to let yourself off the hook.

You're probably pretty compassionate with at least some of the people in your life. Be at least as compassionate with yourself. Forgive yourself and move on. You have a great life to live.

*"When you're different, sometimes you don't see the
millions of people who accept you
for what you are. All you notice is the person who doesn't."*

- JODI PICOULT, CHANGE OF HEART

Day 21:
Stop Seeking Approval

When you do things to make others view you in a certain way, you're sending a message to yourself that the truth is insufficient. You can be kind, but don't be kind just so others will view you as kind. Just be kind.

There's a significant difference between being a good person and a person that wants to be seen as good.

It's okay if you're a little impatient, messy, or don't like the local NFL team. Be honest about who you are. Everyone that loves you will still be around. Anyone you lose doesn't belong in your life anyway.

Prove to yourself that you're good enough just the way you are. It's a much less exhausting way to live, too.

Day 22:
Sit by Yourself

Some people, and you might be one of them, can't stand to be in their own company. They always have to be stimulated by something else. Whether it's the TV, the internet, the radio in the car, or a book, they can't just sit with themselves.

Have you ever wondered why you need those things in your life? The best way to find out why is to take a break from them. The next time you're driving alone, turn off your phone and avoid listening to the radio.

Notice what happens.

With practice, you can be great company for yourself. Instead of avoiding yourself, discover yourself. Sit with yourself for at least 10 minutes each day and see what you discover.

Day 23:
Visit the Doctor and Dentist

It only makes sense that if you make your health a priority, it must mean that you love yourself.

Make appointments with your doctor and dentist for checkups today.

If you're already taking care of this part of your life, make a list of five ways you can be healthier and do at least one of them.

"It's all about falling in love with yourself and sharing that love with someone who appreciates you, rather than looking for love to compensate for a self love deficit."

- EARTHA KITT

Day 24:
Volunteer

It's easier to be happier with yourself when you're helping others. There are plenty of websites that list volunteer opportunities by zip code. Find something that appeals to you and share your time doing something that you think is important.

Even one hour a week can increase the amount of love and compassion you feel for yourself. You'll find that there are other benefits to volunteering, too. Want to know what they are? Go volunteer and find out for yourself.

Day 25:
Sleep

Few things will do more for your health, attitude, and happiness than getting at least seven hours of sleep each night. Even if you think you only need 4-6 hours, try giving yourself a full seven for a week and note the changes in how you feel and function.

Take a nap. Sleep in. Go to bed earlier.

There are times when the best thing you can do to love yourself is to go to bed. You can catch the rerun of Rocky or The Notebook another time.

Make a plan today to squeeze in seven hours of sleep each night for at least a week.

Day 26:
Set and Maintain Boundaries

When you don't love yourself, you put up with a lot of mistreatment. You might be worried that others will be upset or won't like you if you start saying "no" to certain things. Regardless of how hard you try to make everyone happy, you're failing at it.

You can't please everyone, but you can please yourself.

When you tolerate things you don't like, you feel resentful and drained. The solution is to learn to say "no" and be assertive. Let the world know what you need. You'll gain the respect of others and feel better about yourself.

"The best day of your life is the one on which you decide your life is your own.

No apologies or excuses. No one to lean on, rely on, or blame. The gift is yours – it is an amazing journey – and you alone are responsible for the quality of it.

This is the day your life really begins."

- BOB MOAWAD

Do One Thing You Know You Need To Do

Avoid procrastinating on the important things. Whether it's filing your taxes, going to the dentist, or making a tough phone call, just do it. You lose self-respect and self-esteem when you willingly fail to handle your business.

Today, make a list of the things you've been avoiding and get at least one of them done. Then, focus on how good it felt to get that item completed. Imagine how great you would feel in general if you regularly did whatever needed to be done.

Begin making a habit of listing the things you need to do and then doing them.

Day 28:
Trust Your Intuition

You've experienced and seen a lot in your life. You've been successful at some things and less successful at others. It only stands to reason that you now know a lot. Your intuition is based on your experiences.

But do you trust yourself?

Beginning today, trust your intuition more. Start with the small things. Maybe you have an urge to turn right at the stop sign instead of left. Just do it and see what happens.

When faced with a choice. Simply ask yourself, "Which option is the best for me?"

Listen to the answer and do it. Again, see what happens. It would be a shame to put all your experience to waste. You've learned a lot over the course of your life, so put that knowledge and experience to work for you.

Remember that the logical solution isn't always the best solution for you.

Day 29:
Do Something That Makes You Like Yourself More

Volunteering was one example of this, but there are other things you might think that you should be doing, also. It might be going to church, learning a second language, or meditating for an hour each day.

Think about the characteristics you think a person should have. Make a long list. Now, pick one and start doing it.

You might believe that any self-respecting man should be able to change the oil in his car. Or you might believe that everyone should be able to play a musical instrument. Perhaps you believe everyone should have a decent knowledge of world history.

It doesn't matter what it happens to be. It's entirely up to you. Pick something and begin the process. You'll be thrilled with yourself.

"Loving yourself starts with liking yourself, which starts with respecting yourself, which starts with thinking of yourself in positive ways."

- JERRY CORSTEN

Day 30:
Do Something for Someone Else, but Keep it a Secret

This can be a lot of fun, and you'll be quite pleased with yourself. Choose a target. It could be a neighbor, coworker, or random stranger. Do something nice for them.

You might mow their grass, send them a card, or clear the snow off their car. Find a way to do something kind and feel great about yourself for doing it.

Day 31:
Have Fun

Some months have 31 days. Treat this as a bonus.

Do something that's fun today. Go bowling with a few friends. Go to the fancy movie theater and buy that expensive popcorn. You might even go crazy and watch the movie in 3D.

Be silly and do something just because it's fun to you.

"*Love yourself. Enough to take the actions required for your happiness.*

Enough to cut yourself loose from the drama-filled past.

Enough to set a high standard for relationships."

- STEVE MARABOLI

You made it!

You've done a lot to change your perspective of yourself over the last month.

- How do you feel compared to the first day? How would you rate your level of self-love and self-esteem?

- You've been keeping a journal for a few weeks. What has changed in your journal entries over time?

- Do you feel that any of the things you've done have become habits?

- What can you do going forward to further increase your love for yourself?

You should be proud of yourself. Thirty days of learning to love and appreciate yourself is a big achievement, but it's only a small step on a bigger journey.

Loving yourself as much as possible may take a lifetime, but the good news is that you'll only enjoy life more as you learn to love yourself more.

You've learned that the values of the society in which you live doesn't determine your worth. You can set your own criteria.

It's your ability to appreciate yourself and your progress toward your vision of a good person that matters. When you believe that you're becoming a better version of yourself each day, you're going to be pleased with yourself.

Begin thinking about how you can move forward from this new starting point. This is only the beginning of the awesome future that awaits you!

iMarriage

Introduction

our days are filled with meeting new challenges. Your job may require you to work closely with others for long hours. It's normal to get involved in your work, a hobby, or even a friendship outside your marriage.

Sometimes, situations surface that you're unable to predict or control. In essence, many factors exist which can overflow into your marriage. Unfortunately, those factors can wreak chaos on your love and relationship.

How do you manage the rough spots in your marriage? If your marriage was to go on the rocks today, would you know what to do and how to go about fixing it?

This section will help you make it through the difficult times and come out closer and happier than ever before.

Let's look at some common challenges that can strain your relationship with your spouse and how to get past them with your love intact.

Growing Apart

You're likely involved with a number of different activities in an average day: getting the kids off to school, keeping your home and yard in order, and ensuring your family eats well, to name just a few.

When there' s a lot going on, the connections in your important relationships can suffer, especially the closeness of your marriage.

Let's explore what it might look like if you and your spouse begin to grow apart:

1. You're spending less time together. You used to be a real stickler about having dinner together 7 days a week. But you've noticed lately the number has dropped to only 3 or 4 times weekly.

2. You realize you lack knowledge about what your spouse is currently interested in. You used to know when your partner purchased new sports equipment, was reading a book by a new author, or had been getting acquainted with the new neighbors. But now, you're unsure about what your spouse has been doing.

3.   You find yourself not thinking much about your partner. In the past, you couldn't wait to get home to spend some time cooking dinner together or chatting about the latest news story. You wondered off and on throughout your work day what your spouse was up to. But lately, you haven't been thinking much about your partner at all.

Now you know what happens when you grow apart. How can you get back on the same wave length again?

Put these strategies into action if you and your partner have been growing apart:

1.   Start now. Begin today to make an effort to share your feelings about what's happening with you. Your partner will be interested in what you have to say.

2.   Mention you miss having dinner together each day. Your partner will appreciate hearing it and hopefully you'll both make a point of eating together again.

3.   Be flexible. Your partner's work schedule may be an issue. Still, make it clear you miss spending time together.

4.   Plan a specific "date" to just spend time together. It can be an evening this week at home or actually leaving the house together on Saturday for lunch or a long walk.

There are many things you can do to avoid growing apart and staying apart for too long. When you decide you'll walk through life with someone, opening your mind to the many ways you can use to stay close will keep your bond strong.

"A good marriage is like a casserole. Only those responsible for it really know what goes into it."

Disagreement About Handling The Kids

One of the top reasons loving couples experience some bumps in the road to marital bliss is because of the children. Although it's a wonderful blessing to raise children, this blessing is also accompanied by a great deal of stress and hard work.

Not only do children require a lot of your time, but they tend to cramp your social lives. Unfortunately, your kids can sometimes cause a disconnection between you and your partner when it comes to decisions about raising and disciplining them.

Noticing and managing changes in how you get along with your partner, early on after you have kids, will tell the tale of how your marriage will proceed.

Mend fences with your partner now and get on the same team when raising your children:

1. Share your feelings. Tell your partner you've noticed you're having some disagreements about the kids lately. Also state that you want to work them out because you're striving to be on the same page when it comes to raising the kids.

2. Ask questions. Talk with your partner and inquire about what methods he prefers to use when disciplining the kids. Then, listen carefully.

3. Discuss the issues. Agree with your partner when you genuinely share his viewpoints. Next, you can discuss the points that you disagree about and why.

4. Be truthful and ask for what you want. Honestly state what you find upsetting about some of your partner's parenting techniques. Then, ask for what you want. See if you can come to a compromise about how to handle different issues with the children.

> → For example, say something like, "I'm not sure it's helpful to threaten Tommy with spankings because he's beginning to react as if he's afraid of you. Would you consider stopping the threats for a month or so to see if his fear decreases?"

5. Agree to avoid disagreeing in front of the kids. Explain you want to "present a united front" to the children so they see you as a loving team. Plus, you don't want the kids to try to "divide and conquer" their parents.

6.   Suggest attending a local parenting seminar together. State you'd like to do it in the spirit of learning whatever you can about how to be a better parent to your children.

> ⊞ The bonus is that it's an afternoon or evening out together without the kids.

Having kids together will be one of the greatest joys you'll ever experience. Apply these strategies to maintain a strong marital base while you raise your children in harmony.

"A happy marriage is a long conversation which always seems too short."

~ Andre Maurois

Different Ideas about Budgeting and Money

Love and money are often a complicated mix. You've probably each lived alone at some point and managed money exactly like you wanted to.

Perhaps you feel you were doing okay when dealing with finances. So what if you miss a due date every so often or avoid calling back a creditor promptly? You want to enjoy life and you're willing to over-spend to do it.

But maybe you're on the other side of money management: You pay all your bills the day they arrive and you would never open a credit card with an interest rate over 15%. When it comes to money, you're all about saving and putting off gratification.

With the possibility of such different types of money management, you can begin to see how mixing the two styles in a marriage could make for some chaotic times and additional disagreements.

Luckily, there are some easy steps you can take to settle your differences regarding how you manage the family finances.

Apply these tips when discussing money matters:

1. State your concerns. It's wise to avoid letting your feelings about money fester for too long. If you do, your emotions may start to seep into other areas of your life. Start out by sitting down with your partner and saying, "I'd like to talk about two things related to our money situation. I'm concerned about ___."

2. Avoid bringing up finances when you're frustrated or angry. Attempting to state your case diplomatically can be difficult if you're experiencing negative emotions about the topic you wish to discuss.

   → Allow yourself time to be calm before you broach the subject of money.

3. Keep an eye on your speech patterns. Because money can be a sensitive subject, being aware of the volume and tone of your voice will help immensely.

4. Find out your partner's viewpoint. Your spouse may have a specific plan in mind for the future which drives his current money behaviors.

5. Read a good book on personal finance. If there's stress about money affecting your relationship, why not brush up on strategies for managing your cash?

   → Another positive point about educating yourself is it shows your partner you're interested in doing what's best for your family.

→ Plus, if you leave the book lying around where it's easy to see, your partner might just pick it up and read it, too.

6.   Mention your goals for the future. During a money discussion, connect your family' s goals for the future to how you' re handling your money now. This could promote shared goals and a mutual understanding between you and your partner.

→ When you look at the overall picture of your lives together and how it relates to your current money habits, something might "click" for you or your spouse.

7.   Take responsibility for money mistakes you've made. It's tough to admit certain mistakes. Yet, if you refrain from doing so, your partner is left wondering whether you truly see your errors.

→ Your partner might feel apprehensive about living with someone who appears to lack understanding of how their past choices produced unsavory consequences for the family.

→ You could say something like, "I know I made a mistake two years ago when I opened a third credit card account with a high interest rate and ran up the balance. I learned from that experience and I won't do it again."

Even though there are those who say money is the root of all evil, if you just put your heads together, you might discover just the opposite.

You can create the wonderful life you want by working together to successfully manage your finances.

> "In many instances, marriage vows would be more accurate
> if the phrase were changed to, 'until debt do us part.'"
> ~ Sam Irving

There's a Workaholic In The Family

The fast pace of living in the 21st century is exciting, interesting, and ever-changing. Yet it can also push you to work harder for longer periods of time. Sometimes, the work becomes personally rewarding, which is great.

Even still, you or your partner might be a workaholic. And if you are, your relationship can be in for a rough ride.

→ These patterns can alert you to symptoms of your partner being a workaholic:

→ They're hardly ever home for dinner anymore.

→ When they're home or you're out together, they're constantly talking on the phone and texting with their supervisor or co-workers.

→ They seem to want to work overtime much too often.

→ They frequently say they're too tired to take part in family activities.

→ They justify all the work hours they're putting in by saying things like, "I'm earning money for us" or "I'm working toward that promotion."

Did any of those points sound familiar? If so, it may be time to take action and pull your relationship back together.
I was the one in my marriage that was constantly working. I really had to take a step back and figure out how to balance it all.

If you're the one who's developing these workaholic symptoms, you can reverse some of the negative effects on your relationship with these tips:

1. Cap the number of hours you'll work in a day and stick to it. Maybe a 10-hour stint is okay, but a 12-hour day is too long.

2. Control the total number of hours worked weekly. Set limits on the number of hours you'll work in a 7-day period.

3. Limit calls and texts. Establish a few evenings each week (and maybe the weekend, too) where you avoid answering phone calls and texts. Everyone deserves some time off!

4. Apologize and explain yourself. Tell your partner you're sorry for the extra hours you've been working and you were doing it because [the real reason]. Then state what your work plan is for the next 3 to 6 months.

If your partner is the culprit who's overworking, it might be a bit more challenging to confront the situation. However, you do have some options.

Initiate these steps to successfully address your workaholic partner:

1.   Openly acknowledge how you feel about all the extra work hours. Use "I" statements. Review these examples to help you conceptualize this point:

  ⊡ "I'm feeling frustrated because you're gone all the time."

  ⊡ "I miss you—it seems like you're working an awful lot."

  ⊡ "I'm worried because the kids are starting to ask questions about why you're gone so much."

  ⊡ It's perfectly appropriate to express concerns like, "I'm disappointed you're missing a lot of the kids' important activities." Or you could say, "I'd really like you to be more involved with the kids. What can I do to help you be more involved?"

2.   Give your partner advanced notice about special occasions. Notify them in plenty of time when there's a big event coming up and you want them to attend.

> → Mention you realize their work schedule is crammed, but you'd really like them to go to the Family Reunion Barbecue next month.

> → Remind them one or two weeks in advance about your daughter's dance recital or your son's baseball tournament.

3.   Ask how your partner feels about their work schedule. You may discover they're upset, disappointed, or frustrated about their workload too. At least now you are both acknowledging it.

> → If possible, steer the conversation toward problem-solving. Encourage

them to consider what can realistically be done to reduce their work hours.

Although there's nothing shameful about wanting to work hard during certain periods of your life, recognize how being a workaholic can negatively affect your marriage.

When you follow these suggestions, you can rest assured you're doing everything you can to stay close and happy. Hopefully, this will promote a marriage which is healthy and enduring.

elating

Everyone has different communication styles. Think about how well you've communicated with your partner since the beginning of your relationship.

In most relationships, your verbal exchanges evolve over time. Unfortunately, communication styles sometimes deteriorate to the point where it seems like all you're doing is arguing with your spouse.

Put these suggestions into action and quickly put a stop to the arguing:

1. Use a calm and quiet voice. Concentrate on keeping your voice down and your tone pleasant. Nothing can trigger an argument like a loud voice or a defensive tone.

> → Even if you feel you have good reason to be upset, it's rarely effective to speak loudly or with an angry tone in your voice.

2. Do something to disrupt the pattern of arguing. It's up to you to take action and interrupt the destructive cycle of arguing.

> → If your partner says something to you in a loud voice or using highly inflammatory words, make the conscious decision to avoid responding.

→ This is difficult to do because of the nature of arguing. Your partner uses negative language with an "enticingly" argumentative tone of voice and you tend to respond likewise.

→ So, how do you change this response? You do so by changing your behavior to disrupt the pattern.

3.   Decide to be the one who "gives in." Keep in mind your primary goal is to promote harmony in your marriage. So, it's important to be willing to do whatever's necessary. If the issue you're debating about is relatively minor, give in and move on, if at all possible.

4.   Apologize when necessary. It's inconceivable you would do something to upset or emotionally harm your partner (whether you intended to or not) without apologizing for it.

→ If you were the one who'd been wronged, surely you would want your partner to recognize what they did.

→ Likewise, if you have hurt your partner in some way, be mature enough to admit it and say you're sorry.

5.   Forgive. Learn to be generous about forgiving. The reality is we're all human and most of us make plenty of mistakes each day. Don't you want someone to forgive you when you mess up? Since nobody's perfect, forgiving others is important.

→ Even the healthiest of marriages contain episodes of one partner inadvertently hurting the other, apologizing, and then being forgiven by the other.

6.   Avoid holding grudges. Let's say your spouse uses sharp words with you or does something to upset you and they've apologized.

→ Once you accept their apology and forgive them, let go of any hurt and anger you feel.

→ Holding a grudge is a huge block to having a loving relationship. Besides, nothing positive will come from a grudge.

7. Diplomatically discuss long-term wounds you've been distressed about. Perhaps your spouse did something three years ago which hurt you deeply, but you never talked about it. It's quite possible you take every chance to argue because you're struggling to expel the hurt you suffered from that wound.

→ Maybe you should thoroughly discuss the old matter with them, state how you felt at the time, how you've handled those feelings, and then listen to what they have to say about the situation. Take the lead now to work it out!

→ When you communicate openly and honestly, free of negativity, your partner will usually listen. Resolving old wounds, once and for all, will aid you in letting go of your hurt and hopefully tapering your own argumentative behavior.

Once you're conscious of the fact that your words can hurt the ones you love, you can take these steps to change what you've been doing.

These strategies can help make the difference between a struggling, argumentative relationship and a loving, peaceful one.

"The formula for a happy marriage? It's the same as
the one for living in California: when you find a fault,
don't dwell on it."

~ Jay Trachman

Substance Abuse Is Getting In The Way Of Family Harmony

Because substance abuse is rampant in our society, it's imperative to keep your eyes and ears open. Keep this destructive behavior out of your marriage.

Take action and confront the substance abuse by applying these strategies:

1.	Look honestly at your own use of substances. If you're the one using illicit drugs, consider making different choices. If you're taking prescription medication, review the side effects with your doctor to determine whether any of your potential, relationship-disrupting behaviors could be a result of your prescribed medicines.

→ Consider your nicotine habits, alcohol use, and anything else you're ingesting that could affect your emotional state.

2.	Speak to your spouse about their use. In the event it's your spouse who misuses substances, you must tactfully and factually state your concerns when they're not under the influence.

→ Using tact and being factual means you'll have your emotions under control, speak with appropriate voice tone using "I" statements, and factually cite one or two recent situations when their behavior was hurtful, upsetting, or embarrassing to you. Then, express your concern.

3.   Seek drug or alcohol treatment and recovery. If you believe you're caught in an unhealthy cycle of substance use, get professional help immediately.

> → If you think it's your partner facing such a challenge, at the end of your conversation about the issue, state something like, "I'm very concerned and I believe you and I should go for professional help to make our marriage stronger."

Recognize substance abuse is very serious and it can damage or even destroy relationships. However, there are many pathways to recovery.

Supportive people, who are already in recovery, can be found in every community. They want to help. Seek them out if you want guidance, regardless of whether it's you or your spouse who's struggling with substance abuse.

"Marriage is like pi—natural, irrational, and very important."

Lack Of Interest In Your Sexual Relationship

Every marriage will eventually experience a period of time during which the sexual relationship seems to be put on hold. Occasionally, you may be on different wave lengths carnally. Your sexual appetite may be increased while your partner's appears to be waning or vice versa.

Take care of your feelings as a couple by employing these strategies:

1.   Recognize the importance of the sexual connection between you. It's simply a fact: the sexual relationship holds a special place in every marriage.

2.   Acknowledge sexual appetites vary. Even if you lack interest in lovemaking now, remind yourself that your partner may be very interested. If it's the other way around, it's certainly acceptable to let your partner know of your desires.

3.   Talk about it. Interestingly, many couples report they don't speak about their sexual relationship, which means there can be considerable misunderstandings about the topic. As a couple, it's imperative you're able to discuss sex.

> → Specifically, explore how you feel about your lovemaking: what you like and what your partner prefers. Talking about your own sexual relationship can draw you closer and help you understand each other better.

→ Think about what you'd like to share with and know about your partner related to your sexual relationship. Then, find the time to discuss these things with them.

4.   Plan ahead to prime your sexual appetite. It can be titillating for you to think about how you have a "date" on Saturday evening. You'll take the kids to Grandma's to spend the night, go to dinner, and then catch a movie. But returning home alone will be the best part.

5.   Be spontaneous sometimes. Take the lead to initiate sex at times when your partner least expects it.

6.   Develop awareness into your partner's everyday life. Take notice of what your life is like and what your partner's life is like.

→ For example, maybe you're not working overtime and you have all your projects done around the house. You have plenty of energy and time to relax.

→ Now, look at your spouse's situation. Maybe they're working harder than ever to get the kids to all their practices and dance lessons. The house is clean and your partner's doing some volunteer work. When they come in the door, you can see they're exhausted.

➡ Increasing your awareness of how your lives and the demands on each of you fluctuate will increase your understanding of the differences in your carnal desires.

Reviving interest in your sexual relationship can be adventurous and fun. Have an open mind and be willing to experiment with your partner. Cherish the sexual bond you have. Re-discovering the passion you feel for one another can be something you do together all your lives.

> "The Three Ages of Marriage: Twenty is when you watch the TV after. Forty is when you watch the TV during.
> Sixty is when you watch the TV instead."
>
> ~ Unknown

Other Difficult Times That Happen Occasionally

Because marriages occur in "real time," other unexpected situations, like the death of a loved one or job loss, tax our stress levels, patience, and emotions. This sometimes negatively impacts our relationships without warning.

When these difficult times occur, you have to be ready to face the challenges and protect your marriage.

Use these suggestions to keep your marriage solid as a rock during these difficult times:

1. The deaths of family members and close loved ones. It seems uncanny that the death of someone close can actually drive a wedge between couples. Yet, it often happens. But, if you're aware of the relationship disruptions which can occur, you can intervene by applying these tips:

- → Recognize everyone deals with death differently. You may want to talk all the time about the one who passed away, but your partner may find it upsetting to discuss it.

- → Give your partner some space. They may want time to be alone. Take some moments for yourself too, if you desire.

- → Keep the lines of communication open. It might be tough, but it's necessary for you to be able to discuss your emotions with each other periodically through the tough times.

→ Avoid getting angry. If your spouse expresses their grief in a different way than you do, it's okay. Ask for understanding from your spouse if you require some extra support.

→ Spend time together as a couple regularly. Just being in the company of each other can be soothing during times of sadness.

→ Allow time to spend with family and friends. It's comforting to pull together as an extended family in order to support each other in your grief.

2.   One of you experiences a job loss. A job loss can be a profound source of distress between partners. Practice these strategies to come out on the other side stronger and more bonded:

→ Talk about it. If you're the one who lost your job, share your thoughts and feelings verbally. Let your partner know you want to talk about your anger and fears.

→ When your partner suffers a job loss. Go to them and state how you feel. Then, if they haven't yet told you, inquire about what they're thinking and how they're feeling about the situation.

→ Offer and accept support. Demonstrate you've got your spouse's back. Give verbal reassurance each day that you'll both rise to the occasion and get through this together. If your spouse reaches out to comfort you, be accepting and let them know you feel their support. This situation can actually draw you closer and strengthen your bond.

→ State that you are willing to help. Ask what you can do to ease your partner's stress. State you'll go back to work or increase your hours for a while.

Mention you'd see doing these things as an adventure. Besides, you're a team.

→ Discover ways to still have fun together each week. It doesn't cost anything to take a walk, rake leaves, or watch a movie together at home. A job loss shouldn't mean having to sacrifice the fun parts of your relationship. Plus, a relaxing night will clear your mind.

By using these strategies, you can navigate the difficult times together and deepen the love you feel for one another. It's wonderful to know you'll always be there for your partner and they'll always be there for you.

"The great secret of a successful marriage is to treat all disasters as incidents and none of the incidents as disasters."

~ Harold Nicolson

Summary of iMarriage

Your marriage is likely one of the most important relationships you'll have in your lifetime. Experiencing the adventure of a marriage is not for the faint of heart. When you devote your time and energy to your marriage, you'll enjoy some of the most positive experiences ever.

Cherish your marriage and consider it the source of your life, love, and happiness. Why? Because it is.

> "Happily ever after is not a fairy tale. It's a choice."
>
> ~ Fawn Weaver

PARENTING PRINCIPLES:

8 Principles to
Raise Healthy Kids and
Build a Happy Home

INTRODUCTION TO IPARENT

What are the best ways to parent? What are the key principles to keep in mind while fostering a loving family life?

There are key principles you can use to help direct your parenting journey with consistency, love, and structure.

- **Principle #1:** We will discuss the importance of values and expectations in the household. When values inform expectations, everyone in the family can come to a place of understanding and acceptance.

- **Principle #2:** This section covers the importance of boundaries. Having a parent-child relationship is a strong source of guidance for a child.

- **Principle #3:** There are always consequences to our actions. This section covers the importance of teaching your children to take responsibility for their actions. Knowing that actions are followed by consequences will prepare your child for the real world.

- **Principle #4:** It is uncomfortable to allow our children to struggle. However, struggle is a wonderful teacher.

- **Principle #5:** When you have faith in your child's ability, he will feel secure in taking risks. Knowing that you are always on his team will help your child stay motivated when challenges present themselves.

- **Principle #6:** Grateful people are joyful people. By expressing gratitude for each other, your family unit will grow stronger and happier.

- **Principle #7:** Get active with your family. Try new things instead of sticking to the same-old routine. Creating new memories and encouraging new hobbies are two wonderful ways to bond with your child.

- **Principle #8:** Emotional stability and consistency is difficult to maintain. Your children learn these skills from you.

These principles can provide a source of direction in the maze of parenting.

Let's explore these principles together in depth…

PRINCIPLE #1:
WHY YOU NEED FAMILY EXPECTATIONS & VALUES

Creating a consistent household starts with values. Values are sources of strength and direction for everyone in the family. These can dictate the way the family makes decisions together. Values such as authenticity, honesty, respect, and love can flow into every aspect of the family.

Coming up with values as a family is a great way for everyone to take responsibility for living according to these values. Over time, you can gather your family together and reassess the values you follow. As the family evolves, so can the values.

You can choose values by thinking about how you want your family to function. What do you prioritize as a family? How do you want your kids to behave? What do you want them to value as they grow older?

Answering these questions can help you narrow down your core values.

Consider these benefits of implementing values:

1. **Values teach kids to think critically about how they want to behave and navigate through their world.** When you model what it looks like to live according to values, your kids are better able to apply these principles in their own lives. As they face confusing situations and difficult decisions, they'll be able to look to their values and make an

informed decision.

2. **Values implement positive habits.**
   Instead of coming up with expectations out of nowhere, values create a source of expectations. **This can make more sense to kids.** Knowing the importance of acting according to values will teach positive habits based on what they come to value themselves.

   - For example, if they value health, they may develop healthy eating and exercise habits.

3. **Values help kids make decisions for themselves.** When you begin discussing values with your kids, you can show them how they can help guide your decision making. Over time, you can guide them towards choosing things based on their values. Eventually they'll go through that process themselves.

How Can You Put Values To Action?

Having a set of core values helps foster a cohesive family unit. It's important to clarify how to act according to these values.

What does it look like when you're being respectful? Based on that value, multiple expectations can be set up. For example, respect looks like treating the home with respect. So, the expectation might be to keep a clean room.

When kids are old enough to participate in these decisions, they're better able to take ownership of the values and expectations of the household.

If they can set expectations themselves, they're better able to accept the consequences if they do not meet these expectations.

Expectations Provide Structure

Children benefit from having structure. **Though they may resist it at first, setting up family expectations is a valuable piece of the foundation in a household.** The best way to do this is by discussing how you want your values to inform the way your home works.

What does the value of safety look like to you? What do you need to feel safe? Perhaps things such as curfew, driving rules, or treating siblings nicely come into place. Brainstorm as many ideas as you can think of. You can discuss these ideas as new situations present themselves.

Setting Up Effective Expectations

Expectations are most effective when they're achievable. When kids are repeatedly successful, they gain more confidence and pride in themselves. That doesn't mean expectations need to be low. Having reasonably high expectations is not a bad thing. They teach your kids that you believe they're able to meet your standards.

You can expect them to go to science tutoring when you need it, but you don't have to push them to be an astronaut by the time they are nine-years-old.

When children don't have consistent and reliable guidance from their parents, they're more likely to seek out their peers for leadership. This can create a rift between you and your kids and make it more difficult to implement expectations in the future.

Values and expectations are the compass of the family. They help everyone get on the same page about how the family runs. They inform the directions the family takes, and they help sustain closeness as the family evolves.

Expectations let children know what is and is not acceptable. They also teach valuable lessons that kids will carry with them into adulthood.

PRINCIPLE #2: YOU'RE A PARENT, NOT A FRIEND

As children grow older, they begin exploring their own identity. This can lead to a bit of distance between you and your child. This can be hurtful. You have worked so hard and you may sometimes feel unappreciated. Some parents try to connect with their kids by becoming lenient and acting more like a friend than a parent.

Though kids may respond well to this, it actually doesn't benefit them in the long run. **A lack of structure can lead your kids off track.** As a parent, you're responsible for your kid's safety, health, and future. This can seem like a daunting task, but it is possible after you have implemented your values and expectations for your family.

Acting according to your values means setting clear boundaries.

Your kids will test the limits as they try to gain more independence. Having your boundaries in mind as they grow in new directions can help you remain calm and consistent through a tumultuous time.

Set and Stick to Your Boundaries

Follow these strategies to effectively implement boundaries:

- **Begin by evaluating your core values.** Your values tell you what is and is not okay. Just as they help you make decisions and guide your family, they also assist in clarifying boundaries that would otherwise be murky.

- **Have your boundaries ready.** As your kids continue to grow, they'll face new milestones and responsibilities. You don't always have to rescue your kid when they're in difficult situations. You can create boundaries about how much you're willing to help them. This is especially important as kids grow older and need to begin supporting themselves.

- **Pay attention to your feelings and reactions.** When you're in uncharted territory, you'll know a boundary is being crossed if you feel especially angry or uncomfortable. This can help you inform future boundaries when other similar situations occur.

- **Boundaries show that you demand respect.** If you lack self-respect, you're less likely to stand strong when your boundaries are being pushed. Maintaining boundaries helps solidify the expectations you have set into place. **It also creates a healthy dynamic between you and your child.**

Maintain Your Authority

When children don't meet the family expectations, it's time to uphold your values, your boundaries, and your authority. When your kids are testing the limits and begin talking back to you, do your best not to take it personally. If your child is frustrated with you, he may lash out in disrespectful ways. Do your best to keep your cool in these heated situations.

Even though your children are unpredictable and emotional, you can still maintain stability for them by remaining consistent. When you remain calm, your kids will pick up on this. Though thcy may bc going through a difficult time, they will apply what they learn from you to their future situations.

PRINCIPLE #3: BE FIRM, BUT FAIR

You're the first source of knowledge for your kids. It is your job to prepare them for success in the real world. Part of this process means teaching your kids that there are consequences for all of our actions.

You may see your child be friendly to someone and then make a friend. This is a teachable moment where you can show your child that when you are kind and respectful, good things happen. Valuable teachable moments also come about when children do not meet expectations.

Hold the Line

If your child fails a test, you can implement consequences.

Consequences are most impactful when they have a direct relation to the action.

For example, it might not make sense to make your child do the dishes every day for failing a test. Instead, it may be more appropriate to limit free time and increase study time.

This is a good time to teach your child another valuable lesson: we must take responsibility for our actions.

Holding your kids accountable for their actions will teach them to own up to their mistakes in the future. It's helpful to talk through the reasoning behind these consequences so your child understands why she is expected to meet expectations, and what happens when expectations are not met.

This prepares kids for the real world, where consequences can be much worse than getting a bad grade in class for not studying.

Consequences in the Real World

- **Putting in minimal effort leads to less opportunity.** When kids are still living at home, they may get bad grades. You can show your kids that these bad grades will close them off from future opportunities to grow mentally, personally, and professionally. If your kid doesn't apply himself to work in the real world, he may lose his job or miss out on a promotion.

- **Being disrespectful invites disrespect.** If your child doesn't take on the value of respect, he may be careless with others. This will not produce positive relationships. It may lead to your child not being respected professionally or personally. **Teaching your child that you get what you give is a powerful lesson that he will carry into adulthood.**

- **Irresponsibility leads to loss.** If your child is irresponsible with objects, money, or commitments, they're likely to struggle in the future. Being inconsiderate of money could lead to financial struggles in the future. If you teach your child the value of a dollar, he will grow up understanding the importance of saving and spending responsibly.

- **Missing commitments leads to unreliability.** In the real world, if your child does not follow through on what he says he will do, people will likely deem him unreliable. So, when you're teaching your kid to follow through on commitments, you are also preparing him to be available and trustworthy in future endeavors.

Reward Success

Addressing your child when she doesn't meet expectations will help her be more successful in the future, even when she doesn't like the consequences. It's valuable to teach your children about real world consequences. We often jump to the negative when we think of the effects of our actions. However, many of our actions have really positive effects.

Provide specific praise when your child does something successful. You don't have to praise him every time he makes his bed, as that is an expectation. However, you could express genuine appreciation when he takes initiative and cleans the whole house so that you don't have to. Being considerate like this benefits your child in the real world.

Giving rewards for positive behavior is more effective than punishment. It feels good to get praise. Happy brain chemicals such as dopamine are released when we receive praise. Our reward center lights up. This leads to a desire to continue doing good things.

The need for kids to receive praise doesn't mean that you need to overly compliment or coddle them. You don't need to give praise every day (unless your kid is on a real winning-streak). In fact, giving praise constantly makes it less valuable. Your child may begin to *expect* praise.

You don't need to give praise every day, and you don't need to wait six months between each time you express appreciation for your child's behavior. Instead, **give praise when it's appropriate.**

For example:

- When your child has gone above and beyond expectations

- When he has taken initiative for himself

- When she has completed a particularly challenging task

This type of encouragement is motivating and will help your child believe in his capabilities.

The praise you give should be intentional and specific.

For example, instead of saying, "You got an A, good job." You can say, "Wow, I see that you worked very hard to achieve this. You asked for help and you persevered through the obstacles. You have a strong work ethic."

Talk About It

Using positive action as a teachable moment leads to more positive actions from your kids. When paired with natural consequences for negative actions, **your child will have a better idea of how his actions affect his world and the world of those around him.**

Having conversations in these moments is valuable. You can think through your child's behavior with her. It may even give you a better understanding of why she behaved the way she did.

Have the difficult conversation.

If your child failed a test, you may have noticed that he had hardly studied. The instinct is to say, "Well, you need to study more." That's probably true. However, having a conversation about this could broaden your understanding of a larger issue.

Maybe his math class is really hard to understand and he feels embarrassed. Fear of failure often leads to less effort. Children are afraid of trying something and failing anyway.

Instead, they can put forth little effort and say, "Well, I failed that test because I didn't study, not because I'm not smart."

Once you're able to have a conversation about this issue, you can have a better idea of how to proceed.

Instead of punishing your child, you can teach him what to do when he needs help. Require that he meet with his teacher once a week or get him a tutor.

Punishing a behavior that a child doesn't know how to fix can lead to confusion and resentment instead of progress.

Remaining firm but fair requires clear expectations and boundaries.

Natural consequences are implemented because that's how the real world operates. Similarly, outstanding behavior merits positive praise and acknowledgement.

Having a conversation about the consequences at hand can teach both you and your child something new. It can even lead to a better understanding of the needs of your child.

PRINCIPLE #4: MISTAKES ARE OKAY

Life is in a constant flow of success and failure, of happiness and disappointment. This is the nature of life. It is uncomfortable and difficult, but going through difficulty builds resilience. If you find that your child has made a mistake, you may want to comfort them and solve the problem for them.

Let your child hold the tension.

This will continue to help them take responsibility for their actions. When they're able to feel the feelings that go along with making the mistake, they'll be able to evaluate their values and learn what it feels like when they are or are not acting in accordance with those values.

When you come in to save the day when something goes wrong, your child will begin to think that he can't solve problems without you. This could lead to feelings of helplessness and doubt in the future.

When you let your child have ownership of the mistake, you teach them that you know they can handle it.

When To Step In

Let your child fail safely.

When your child is about to make a mistake that you know will cause harm, it's valuable to step in sooner rather than later. Kids don't have fully-developed frontal lobes in their brains. This means they're not fully able to think through the consequences of their actions. Sometimes you need to point this out to them and have a conversation.

You can give guidance when your child asks for help. Part of making mistakes means learning how to ask for help. If your child reaches out for help, you can guide him in the right direction. In fact, these can be valuable moments of communication and understanding.

You don't need to give more help than your boundaries permit. However, when it's appropriate you can provide assistance.

Foster Independence

If your child makes a mistake, it means she was trying to make a decision for herself and her own individuality. That's a good thing! When you make all of the decisions for your child, she won't feel comfortable to navigate failure and learn from it.

When failure comes in the real world, she'll feel helpless and lost rather than well-equipped to handle any difficulties.

If you can teach your child to grow through mistakes at an early age, she will know the coping skills she needs to handle anything in the future.

Looking for solutions to problems happens in the midst of problems. You don't need to leave your child out in the wild alone, but you don't need to hold her hand, either. You can find a happy medium and be a source of wisdom while your child is gaining her own wisdom.

Going through trials and tribulations builds character and compassion. By experiencing failure, your child can better connect with the authentic human experience.

Though you don't need to coddle your children through their mistakes, you also do not have to give up on them. If you give up on your child, he will likely sense this negativity and respond adversely to it.

PRINCIPLE #5: KIDS WILL BE AS SUCCESSFUL AS YOU BELIEVE THEY CAN BE

It can be disappointing and frustrating when kids don't meet the expectations you've set out for them based on your values. When the same mistake is repeated over and over again, you may begin to lose hope. It's natural to begin thinking of your child in a less positive light.

For example, if your child continuously does poorly in school, you may begin to think of him as a poor student. It may be true that your child struggles frequently. However, when you begin to think of him as a bad student, he will see himself that way, too.

Treating him like he's going to fail or have another bad semester will often be a self-fulfilling prophecy. Treating your child as though he has already failed is not likely to lead to success.

A Self-Fulfilling Prophecy

There was once a study done at a school where teachers were given two different groups of students:

- The teachers were told that Group A was a group of bad influences and students who struggle. Unbeknownst to the teachers, this group was actually comprised of high-achievers.

- Group B was said to be a group of outstanding students with good behavior. In fact, the opposite was true.

The study found that teachers treated these groups of students differently. Teachers treated these students according to their beliefs about how successful these students were going to be.

As a result, the previously high-performing students in Group A began having behavioral issues and doing poorly in school. The previously less-successful students began performing better in school and earning better grades.

As you can see from the study, making assumptions about the potential of children causes their behavior to change.

Even though they are not specifically told, "You're not well-behaved," children will pick up on the ways that you treat them according to this belief. Over time, they'll begin believing this themselves and will begin to act out even more.

For your best results, use these strategies to show support:

1. **Remember that if you begin to doubt your child, he will begin to doubt himself.** Though it may sometimes seem hopeless, staying optimistic will encourage your child to keep trying. When you give up, your kid does, too.

2. **Set high expectations and pay attention to the outcome.** When your child is struggling through a mistake, help him identify his situation and think positively about solutions. Encourage conversations about other possible outcomes and goals.

3. **Lead by example.** When you show your child that you believe in yourself, he will learn what it looks like to persevere through difficulty.

Your Child is Capable

Children are observant and curious. They're capable of learning great new things everyday, and they do. When they sense what you feel about them, they're more likely to perform according to your predictions.

Let your child explore new things and learn as they go.

Perhaps your child has a large interest in soccer. Despite his love of the sport, he may trip over the ball in every game. Instead of encouraging him to give up, show him that you believe in his ability to develop greater skills in something he is dedicated to.

Instead of shaming him when he doesn't make that game-winning goal, you can instead encourage him to keep practicing. This will show him that you believe him. **It will motivate him to continue making an effort.**

This will be a valuable skill later in life when difficulties arise. Instead of retreating while approaching hurdles, your child will learn to approach them with courage. With willingness to work through struggle, anything is possible.

As children grow and evolve, their optimism will grow in proportion to your belief in their success.

Though it isn't always easy to maintain a positive spirit in times of difficulty, an effort must be made to move forward with hope.

When you believe in the potential of your child, he will, too. This positive thinking benefits gratitude. And, gratitude increases positive thinking. There is no replacement for a strong daily practice of gratitude.

PRINCIPLE #6: FOSTER A GRATEFUL HEART

Practice gratitude each day – both alone and with your family. Practice gratitude every day. Just 15 minutes of gratitude each day has many benefits that grow from your heart, to the heart of your family, and on to your community.

Our society tends towards the negative. Things are frequently inconvenient or disappointing. That is not the lens through which you want to see your world, however. Instead, make a conscious effort to increase your gratitude skills.

Extensive research has shown many benefits of gratitude. Gratitude increases feelings of connectedness and peace. Not only will the bond of your family grow stronger, but each member of the family will benefit as well.

Consider these benefits of gratitude:

1. **Gratitude helps develop empathy. When we're grateful, we're more aware of others and less concerned with ourselves.** We have a broader understanding of the world around us. As a result, we're better able to be patient and understanding with others.

2. **Gratitude enhances feelings of joy.** Even when the storms of life present themselves, grateful people are able to remain hopeful. **Gratitude cultivates a core feeling of joy that is not evaporated in times of stress.**

3. **We sleep better when we're grateful.** By ending your day with gratitude, you're less likely to ruminate on the negative aspects of your day. If you're able to see

the goodness and express gratitude, you'll feel stronger feelings of peacefulness.

4. **Gratitude builds resilience.** By actively acknowledging the specific things that you're grateful for, you're a making positive effort to look on the bright side. **Life is less likely to keep you down when you're able to see the light through the fog.**

5. **Gratitude increases self-compassion and decreases negative self-talk.** When we're able to step back and look at the positive, our thoughts are likely to mimic that positivity. This will lead to more positive self-talk and forgiveness in future errors.

Gratitude in Action

It's one thing to think about and appreciate the idea of gratitude. It's a different thing entirely to put that gratitude into action. You may want to be grateful, but are not sure how.

You can start by noticing positive aspects of your day. At the end of each day, ask yourself, "What was my favorite thing about this day?"

Start small and work your way up to paying more attention to gratitude. When you're able to express gratitude in a meaningful way, you'll reap all of the benefits of a consistent gratitude practice.

By practicing gratitude as a family, you can teach your children to be grateful independently.

Here are some ways you can practice gratitude as a family:

1. **Create a family happy jar.** Grab a jar and a stack of index cards. At the end of each day, have everyone write down one thing they're grateful for about the day on an index card. All of you can share what you're grateful for and then put your index cards in the jar. Date the cards so

you can look back at all your happy memories!

2. **Talk about three things you're grateful for.** On the way to school or over breakfast, list three things you're grateful for. Ask your children to do the same. You can all begin your day with gratitude and gain a positive outlook on the day.

3. **Write thank you notes.** Show your children the importance of expressing thanks by sending thank you cards. Whether you're grateful for a vacation, a gift, or an opportunity, a thank you card is always appropriate. **This will teach your kids to really think about their gratitude.**

By spending time in gratitude, you'll feel a peace with the present moment that is hard to achieve any other way. When you can accept and be grateful for what you have in the moment, you'll feel at ease with your family.

PRINCIPLE #7: BE ACTIVE, NOT PASSIVE

Building a happy home and healthy children requires an intentional effort from every member of the family. It's easy to turn on Netflix and have a day where you don't have to pay attention to anything. Some days, that really is exactly what you need.

Pay attention to how your family spends time together. If you notice that you're mostly inside or not doing many activities as a family, make a point to dedicate time with family.

Invest in Memories

Invest in memories that bring your family closer together. You can get outside and participate in activities with your family.

Quality time is a great way to display love for your children.

Paying attention and listening to them can help build their confidence. It can also help you get to know your children as they grow and develop.

By fostering strong familial relationships, interpersonal skills are strengthened outside of the household. Children don't forget cherished one-on-one time. Family bond is a foundational component in the development of a well-rounded child.

A secure relationship is one where both parties feel known, understood, and accepted.

Showing your child that you take her seriously and care about who she is helps her develop a secure attachment. This will make your child feel comfortable taking risks and trying new things.

When she knows she has a supportive family encouraging her, she is comfortable in challenging situations.

Fostering these positive relationships requires time and creativity. A good place to start is by taking the dogs for a walk together or going out to dinner together. Doing these activities without cell phones can present new opportunities for connection.

Making unique memories will bring about even more ways to connect.

Try these fun family activities:

1. **Choose your family's favorite non-profit and spend a day volunteering together.** Being of service increases empathy and gives a broader perspective of the world. Volunteering helps the family grow together. It also teaches your children the importance of compassion for others.

2. **Visit a museum.** Going to a museum provides the opportunity to have their own experience, together. As each of you interpret the art around you, you can have interesting conversations that may lead to new knowledge and understanding of each other. Seeing art and creativity in action can inspire creativity for everyone in the family.

3. **Learn something new together.** Take an art or cooking class. If you go to a painting class together, you can each create something new and have fun embracing the new experience. Taking a cooking class leads not only to innovation in the kitchen, but the chance to teach your kids about valuable life skills.

4. **Have an adventure together.** Get out of the house and go on a hike or a nice walk. Getting away from screens and other worldly distractions can help you take a step back and just be together as a family. Family exercise promotes a healthy lifestyle and emphasizes the importance

of long term physical health.

5. **Play games.** Partake in the hobbies that your children love. If you don't know much about their hobby, ask questions and get curious. **You will learn more about your children's strengths and interests. Your child will feel respect and love in return.**

Beginning habits of family time will hold the family closer together during times of stress or uncertainty. It's easy to let time fly and get stuck in the hustle and bustle of daily life. By adding regular family time to your weekly routine, your family will be able to stay in touch and strengthen communication.

As your kids turn to teens and teens turn to young adults, you'll remain closer by spending consistent time together.

You'll have the joy of watching your kids grow up by taking them out and encouraging them to pursue things that are interesting to them. When you guide them to new experiences, they'll become more curious about the world around them.

PRINCIPLE #8: TEACH EMOTIONAL INTELLIGENCE

Emotional intelligence is defined as *"the capacity to be aware of, control, and express one's emotions, and to handle interpersonal relationships judiciously and empathetically."*

This skill is one that is carefully crafted. Teaching this skill is not easy – it requires allowing vulnerability and truth.

If your child is the smartest person in the room but has a hard time relating to people emotionally, he is less likely to move forward than an emotionally intelligent person. The ability to connect with others in a vulnerable and authentic way is a carefully crafted skill that your child will learn from you.

Daniel Goleman is one of the key innovators in the research on emotional intelligence. He has written a number of books on the topic. In them, he outlines the five key elements of emotional intelligence.

Five key elements of emotional intelligence:

1. **Genuine emotional intelligence begins with self-awareness.** Self-awareness is an ability to recognize emotions and see their impact on those around you. Those who have an ability to understand the sources of their emotions are better able to understand how their emotions are affecting their current state of mind.

2. **Self-regulation leads to adaptability and acceptance of change.** Regulating emotions can only happen with a strong sense of self-awareness. **Self-regulation**

means knowing when and how to express emotions. The ability to remain calm in stressful situations until you are in a safe place to process your feelings is the core of self-regulation.

3. **Motivation should come from inside rather than outside sources.** Rather than chasing fame and recognition, intrinsically motivated people work hard in order to fulfill their own goals and expectations. Those who are motivated from secure sources are better able to roll with the punches and adapt to new things. They are always looking for ways to improve and learn new things.

4. **Empathy is unequivocally linked to emotional intelligence.** This is the skill that most helps in connection with other people because it entails an ability to understand the struggles and success of those around them. By being able to connect with a diverse range of people, empathetic people foster stronger and

more authentic connections to others.

5. **Social skills develop emotional intelligence and emotional intelligence develops social skills.** An ability to be positive and uplifting in daily social interactions improves relationships with the people you come into contact with.

Teach with Heart

Teaching emotional intelligence may be the most valuable thing you can pass on to your child. However, it can also be the most difficult because it requires you to get vulnerable and honest in front of your child to an appropriate extent. Though it may sound cheesy, talking about feelings cannot be replaced with any other activity.

The ability to identify feelings starts early and it starts with you. You can begin teaching your child about feelings at a young age by expressing your own feelings.

For example, you can say, "When you don't follow my directions about crossing the street, I feel scared that you'll get hurt by a car." **By showing your child that you're scared and hurt instead of strictly reprimanding him, the experience will teach him more about safety.**

Non-Judgmental Communication

Pausing to identify your emotions is a difficult task. It's especially difficult in front of children. They look up to us and we often feel pressure to be the perfect parents they deserve. No parents are perfect.

The biggest thing children deserve is authenticity and truth from their parents. Grown-ups who can admit their human-ness are teaching a valuable lesson in honesty.

Communicating your feelings teaches your kids to communicate their feelings, too. **Instead of acting out of anger, having a conversation about it is much more productive**. Talking through feelings and getting to a place of understanding teaches healthy habits.

Trust is built when you allow your children to confide in you. When they're young, they are experiencing new emotions at every turn. Uncharted territory can be challenging to navigate. If you can listen without judgment, your child will feel more secure and willing to be honest.

When people can communicate their feelings instead of blowing up in rage or acting passive aggressive, they are more likely to get through their difficulty in a reasonable time frame.

Encourage Curiosity

It's difficult to experience new and uncomfortable emotions.

From the first hangnail to the first heartbreak, each hurdle that life brings requires more resilience and emotional understanding. Having conversations about these hurdles promotes emotional growth and understanding of self.

When you're going through your own exploration of emotions, you can share what the process is like with your child. When difficulties arise in your child's life, you don't need to swoop in to save the day. Instead, **sit with your child and encourage him to dive into his emotions with curiosity.**

Instead of running from emotions, show your children how to cope with and feel through life's many emotions.

Teach Coping Skills

It's not always easy to let emotions flow through and out of us. Instead, the instinct is usually to try to hold it together and feign stability. Rather than covering up authentic emotions, teach your kids to feel and cope with these emotions in healthy ways.

When children don't know how to feel emotions, they often turn to other sources for a mental escape and relief. There are many coping skills online that are available for all personality types. When you're first introducing coping skills to your child, try them together and see what works.

Try these fun and effective coping skill activities:

1. **Observe nature.** After a particularly difficult day, spend time in nature in order to focus on what is right in front of you rather than negative ruminations.

2. **Have a dance break.** Take a moment to let loose and be silly in the midst of difficult times. Put on a favorite song and let your dancing shoes take over. This can help give a moment of relief in some

murky waters.

3. **Create art.** Whether the interest is in woodworking or scrapbooking, choosing some materials and getting creative is effective in entering a calm state of mindfulness.

4. **Practice Gratitude.** Fostering a grateful heart comes in handy in more ways than one! Gratitude increases feelings of peace. It helps connect us to what is around us in the present moment and it helps ease the pain of difficult stress.

SUMMARY IPARENT

There's no perfect way to parent.

Having children means embracing the unpredictability of life. When you have principles to help guide the way you raise your kids and build your family, you're better able to stay consistent throughout the ebbs and flows of life.

Your family will grow with each passing year. Just as your kids will experience growing pains as they grow taller, your family will go through growing pains as you learn new lessons together. With every endeavor comes missteps, wrong turns, and entirely wrong directions.

When your values are clarified, a strong foundation of guidance provides an anchor when everything feels up in the air. These values help clarify the expectations by which you and your family operate.

By acting according to values, you'll raise children into adults who also have their own set of values. Clarity of values provides a canvas on which to build a life one can be proud of. The benefits of these values present themselves and foster a stronger ability to implement positive habits and think positively.

Set expectations that are both challenging and achievable.

Based on your values, you can decide on the way you expect each member of your family to behave. Allow your children to be a part of this conversation and decide upon consequences that are related to the expectation.

Make the line between peer and parent very clear.

Though it is tempting to be well-liked rather than respected, remember that you're a parent and not a friend. This doesn't mean you can't get along with or have fun with your child. **It does mean you need to have clear boundaries.**

Boundaries help solidify expectations and they clarify the consequences of behavior. You may sometimes get a negative reaction from your child when they're faced with frustration towards you. Part of your job is to teach stability in times of anger or disagreement. You can model this with your child by remaining calm and patient.

Prepare your child for the real world by teaching him about the natural consequences of behavior. **Remain both consistent and considerate – firm, but fair.**

When your child knows the importance of taking responsibility for his actions, he will be cognizant of his behavior.

Remind your child of the real-life consequences of his behavior by providing consequences to negative behavior that are related to the event. For example, if your child steals from someone, a corresponding consequence may including making verbal and financial amends.

Reward above-and-beyond behavior with positive praise and acknowledgement. Think of a specific success and outline the qualities that helped your child get that success.

Talk before you punish.

When your child does not meet your expectations, consequences follow naturally. However, before implementing these consequences be sure to have a conversation about the issue. Your child may have a different view of the situation.

If you can communicate with your child about his consequences, he is better able to make informed decisions in the future.

Let your children take risks and find their own way through mistakes.

You're responsible for your child's health and safety. You are not responsible for saving your child from every failure and hurdle they face. Encourage him to take responsibility for himself by looking at the mistake he has made and learning what he can from it.

Step in when your child is in danger or suffering. As your child gets older, you can put more responsibility on her to ask for help and find her way to her own solution. **Look to your values to direct you in times of distress for your child.**

Letting your child learn from failure does not mean giving up hope.

Your child will be as prosperous and successful as you believe he can be. When you believe in the potential of your child, she will, too. When you act as though your child will be successful, he will feel encouraged to meet those expectations.

If you notice consistent missteps, it may be more difficult to maintain patience and hope. However, these are the times when your child needs you to believe in him the most.

Teach gratitude, live gratefully.

Intentionally choosing 15 minutes per day being grateful has numerous benefits. It lowers stress levels and increases empathy. Gratitude helps improve sleep patterns and it nurtures self-compassion.

Expressing gratitude of your family helps strengthen the familial bonds between each member of the family. When we are grateful, we are more aware of the present moment and we enjoy the company of our loved ones on a deeper level.

Invest in memories, not TVs.

Step away from screens and take an active role in your family and create happy memories with unique experiences. Learn something new, be of service, or just act silly and have fun by playing games. These precious bonding moments cannot be replaced.

Emotional intelligence is a key to a loving and supportive household.

The ability to identify emotions and express them appropriately is a skill that is best taught by you. Your children will learn how to behave emotionally based on the way you regulate your own emotions. You can have honest conversations with your child about true emotions.

When difficult emotions present themselves, you can help them gather a collection of coping skills that they can use in future times of fear or confusion.

Choose your priorities, imagine your happy family, and take action. Raising healthy kids and building a happy home comes from your heart and permeates every member of your family. Enjoy the love and support of a healthy family while implementing new skills to help your family grow and move forward together.

Made in the USA
Columbia, SC
19 January 2025

51083886R00083